Can You Fly High, Wright Brothers?

Melvin and Gilda Berger
illustrated by Brandon Dorman

SCHOLASTIC NONFICTION
an imprint of
SCHOLASTIC

Contents

Who were the Wright brothers?

The Wright brothers were Wilbur and Orville Wright. They made history by building and flying the first airplane powered by an engine. Their first successful flight took place on December 17, 1903.

Within a few years, airplanes completely changed the world. Early airplanes fought battles in World War I (1914–1918) and delivered mail over big distances. Later, planes carried people around the globe and did many other jobs, from fighting forest fires to spraying crops.

Airplanes have changed a lot since the Wright brothers' invention. Yet modern planes still work much like the first airplane. From 1903 to today, the sky's the limit!

Orville (left) and Wilbur (right) in their hometown of Dayton, Ohio. This photo was taken in 1909 after they became famous for inventing the airplane.

Who was the older brother?

Wilbur Wright was older than Orville. He was born on April 16, 1867, at a farm near Millville, Indiana. Wilbur was the third son of Milton and Susan Wright. The father was a minister and later a bishop. His church duties sent him to different parts of the country. To stay together, the family moved often.

People said that young Wilbur was quiet and serious like his father.

Wilbur at age twelve.

Milton Wright

Susan Wright

Wilbur enjoyed reading and studying. He spoke slowly and rarely got angry.

In other ways, Wilbur was like his mother. Susan Wright was busy, active, and very good at fixing things. While her husband was away, Mrs. Wright ran the house and took care of the children. Wilbur helped his mother and became good at home repairs.

How much younger was Orville Wright?

Orville Wright was born four years after Wilbur, on August 19, 1871. By that time, the family was living in Dayton, Ohio.

Orville was more fun-loving than Wilbur.

He spoke fast and enjoyed telling jokes. He often played tricks on people. His bubbly personality led Orville's friends and family to call him Bubbo.

Orville at age eight.

As a child, Orville was very curious, but not too interested in school. His favorite activity was taking things apart and discovering how they worked. Then he liked to put them back together again.

Orville and Wilbur's older brothers were named Reuchlin and Lonn. Their sister, Katharine, was born three years after Orville. When their mother died, Katharine was fifteen years old. She kept house for her brothers and father until she left for college.

Katharine at age four.

Did the Wright brothers have happy childhoods?

The Wright children grew up in a home that was strict, but very loving. Their parents encouraged the children to follow their own interests and always ask questions. The children had many books and the brothers did lots of reading.

The Wright family home in Dayton, Ohio in 1900. What do you see leaning against the front fence?

Wilbur once said, "From the time we were little children, my brother Orville and myself lived together, played together, worked together, and, in fact, thought together." The brothers were so close that they would often finish each other's sentences!

Together, Wilbur and Orville made a good team. Wilbur usually thought up things they could make. Then Orville, with Wilbur's help, built the objects from scraps of wood or metal they found around the house.

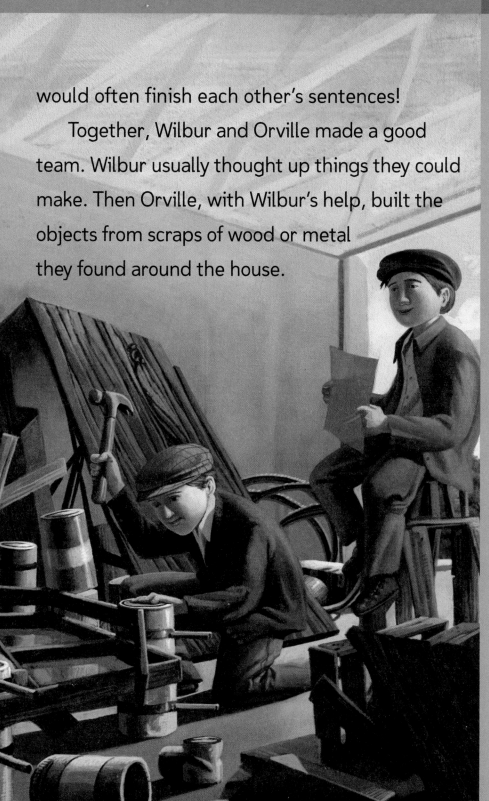

When did the brothers become interested in flying?

When Wilbur was eleven and Orville was seven, their father brought home a surprise. It was a toy helicopter. The plane was powered by a rubber band attached to two propellers. Twisting the rubber band made the propellers spin and sent the helicopter up into the air.

The boys spent hours playing with this toy. They named it "the Bat." When the Bat broke, they were able to fix it right away. The brothers also made copies of the Bat and earned money selling the toys to their friends.

Later, the brothers tried to build a larger toy helicopter. But they could not get it to fly. Wilbur and Orville said their interest in flying started with the Bat — and the trouble they had making a larger helicopter.

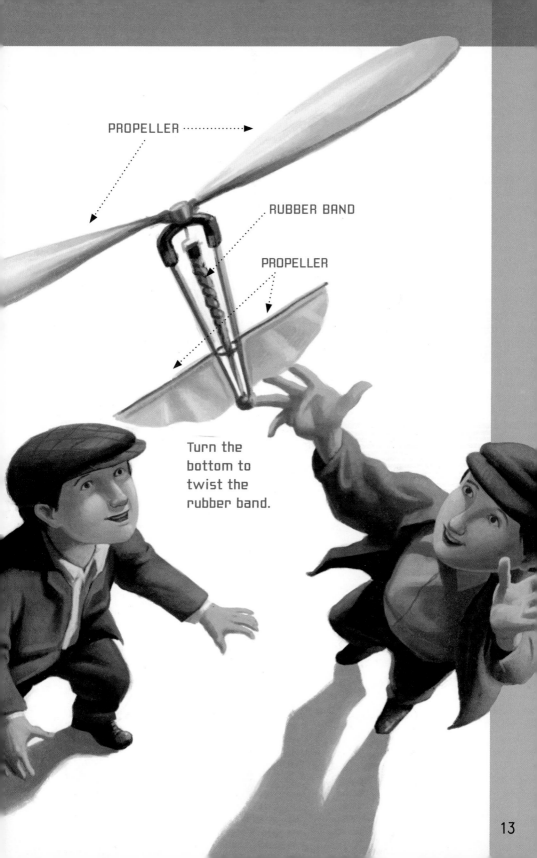

PROPELLER

RUBBER BAND

PROPELLER

Turn the bottom to twist the rubber band.

Did the Wright brothers go to college?

Orville and Wilbur were average students. However, neither of them graduated from high school. Orville dropped out before graduation, and Wilbur never took his final exams.

Wilbur thought about going to college, but an accident changed his mind. He was badly hurt playing ice hockey. His recovery took four years. During that time, Wilbur also took care of his mother, who was very sick. After that, he decided to stay at home. Instead of going to college, both brothers made up their minds to start a business.

In this high school class picture, Orville is standing in the center of the last row of students. Orville's friend, Paul Laurence Dunbar (left rear), later became a famous poet. Soon after this picture was taken, Orville dropped out of school and began to work in the printing business.

What was the Wright brothers' first business?

Orville got interested in the printing business when he was helping his father in the church printing plant. At thirteen, he built his own printing press — with help from Wilbur. Orville made the press out of scrap metal, an old tombstone, and firewood!

At first, Orville and Wilbur put their homemade printing press to work doing small printing jobs for friends. Later, they published a weekly newspaper called the *West Side News*.

The first issue came
out on March 1, 1889.
Wilbur was twenty-one;
Orville was seventeen.

After a year, Orville
and Wilbur changed the *West
Side News* to a daily newspaper.
But three months later the paper failed.
The brothers went back to being printers.
They mostly made business cards, wedding
invitations, and posters.

Letter blocks
used in printing
presses.

IDE NEWS.

N. OHIO, MAY 25, 1889

forsaking all others, cleave only
unto her, so long as you both shall
live!"

The minister paused for the re-
sponse. The groom hung down
his head, and was silent, but the
bride, in a staccato tone, exclaim-
ed, "Yes, sir, I'll see to it that he
does all that!"

It was evident who would rule in
that household. But a Scotch
clergyman once warned a groom
who insisted upon promising to
obey his wife. The clergyman,
while traveling through a village,
was requested to officiate at a
marriage, in the absence of the
parish minister. Just as

No. 12

The best, the cheapest and the
Safest place to buy a PIANO or ORGAN
is at

Martin Bros. & Fritch,
W Fourth St, Kuhns Block

Telephone 399.

JOHN M NUTT

Attorney at Law,
Rooms 1 and 2 Kuhns Building

Remember that

Wilbur was
editor and
Orville was
publisher
of the *West
Side News.*
Notice the
advertisements
on the right-
hand side.

17

What did the Wright brothers do next?

In the 1890s, a new fad was sweeping the country. It was bicycles. The old kind had giant front wheels and tiny back wheels. The new ones looked like the bikes of today. They were safer and easier to ride.

Wilbur and Orville were among the first in Dayton to own the new bicycles. Wilbur enjoyed going for long rides into the country. Orville was more interested in racing. Of course, both brothers were able to fix their bikes when anything went wrong.

Soon, people began asking Wilbur and Orville to repair their bikes. By 1892, the

The Wright brothers' bicycle store, called the Wright Cycle Company, in Dayton.

Wright brothers decided to close the printing shop and open a bicycle store. They sold, fixed, and rented bikes — and even began building their own bicycles.

When did Wilbur and Orville decide to build an airplane?

The brothers first got the idea of inventing an airplane in 1896. They read a newspaper article about the German inventor Otto Lilienthal. He was testing a glider when it crashed and he was killed. (A glider is an aircraft that looks something like a small airplane — but without an engine. It is held up by wind and air currents.)

Soon the brothers were reading all they could about flying. They found that people had long dreamed of soaring like birds. Around the year 1485, Leonardo da Vinci imagined a flying machine with flapping wings.

Others built giant balloons filled with hot air that rose up into the sky. Many

Leonardo da Vinci's drawing shows an experiment to test the power of a wing.

built gliders. But no one had built a safe and useful flying machine. The Wright brothers decided to give it a try!

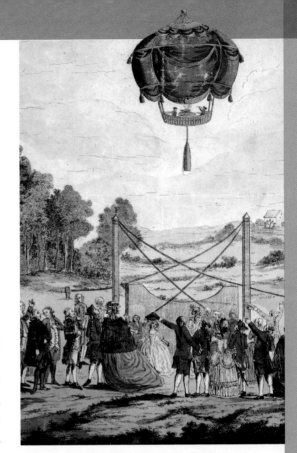

An illustration of the first manned hot-air balloon ride, made in 1783 by the French Montgolfier brothers. Originally, hot-air balloons were slow and dangerous.

A side view of a glider flying as a kite. Wilbur (left) and Orville (right) are holding the long cords that are attached to the tips of the kite's wings. On the kite was in the air, they steered it by lowering one wing or the other

Why did the Wrights build a giant kite?

First, the Wright brothers built a giant kite shaped like a glider. They wanted to find a way to steer it. No one had yet solved this problem with flying machines.

Wilbur studied how birds fly. Birds raise one wing and lower the other to make a turn. Could the Wrights steer the kite by twisting its wings?

The Wrights ran cords from the kite's wingtips to small sticks that they held in their hands. When the kite was in the air, they pulled on the right cord. The kite turned to the right. When they pulled on the left cord, the kite turned to the left. It worked!

A modern box kite resembles the Wright brothers' glider.

What happened after that?

Next, the Wright brothers built a glider big enough to carry one person. They put it together at their Dayton bicycle shop. It had two wings, one above the other. The glider's wooden body was covered with white cotton cloth.

The pilot lay down on the lower wing. His feet rested against a wooden bar. Wires connected the ends of the bar to the wingtips. By pushing with one foot, the glider turned to the left. By pushing with the other foot, the glider turned to the right.

In front of the bottom wing was a flat panel that the brothers called the elevator. The pilot controlled the elevator with his hands. By raising or lowering the elevator, the pilot made the glider go up or down.

Orville flies in this glider big enough to carry a person. The brothers were getting closer to building and flying a powered airplane.

How does a glider fly?

A glider flies when the air under the wings pushes up harder than the air above pushes down.

A glider's wings are curved on top and flat on the bottom. The shape of a glider's wing is important when the glider is moving.

As the glider moves forward, the air flowing above the wings flows faster than the air flowing under the wings. Fast-moving

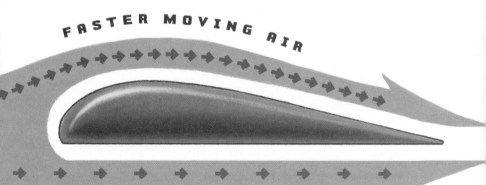

FASTER MOVING AIR

SLOWER MOVING AIR

air does not press down as hard as slower-moving air presses up.

To get off the ground, the glider must be moving quite fast. Gliders get up to speed by rolling down a hill or by being towed. At the right speed, the stronger air pressure beneath the wings lifts the glider and holds it up in the air.

This is a modern-day glider. Notice the pilot on the inside.

Try it out!

Experiment #1: See how air pressure can hold things up.

You'll need a straw and a glass of water.

1. Push the straw into the water. Water goes into the straw.

2. Cover the top of the straw with your fingertip.

3. Raise the straw above the glass.

The water stays inside! Why?

Air presses in all directions: up, down, and on all sides. Your finger on the straw stops the air from pressing down on the water. The air pressure under the water is now stronger than the air pressure above. Air pressure holds up the water — just as air pressure holds up a glider or airplane.

Try it out!

Experiment #2: See how fast-moving air presses less hard than slow-moving air.

You'll need a piece of paper, a ruler, and a pair of scissors.

1. Cut a piece of paper about 1 inch (2.5 cm) wide and 7 inches (17.8 cm) long.

2. Hold one end just below your lower lip.

3. Blow gently across the paper.

The paper strip rises up! Why?

The air speeds across the top of the paper faster than the air below the paper. The air under the paper pushes up harder than the fast-moving air above the paper presses down. The paper rises.

When did the Wright brothers test their glider?

The first test took place in the summer of 1900. The brothers shipped the glider to Kitty Hawk, North Carolina, on the Atlantic coast. Kitty Hawk is on a strip of land with big sand hills called dunes. The glider could pick up speed rolling down a dune. And, in case of a crash, the sand would cause less damage. Also, winds blow there all the time. They would help the glider fly.

Each day, the brothers made at least a dozen flights. The best ones lasted just a few seconds and covered only a few hundred feet (meters).

In 1901 and 1902, the brothers built two more gliders. They made thousands of test flights. Finally, they were ready to move on.

Two men guide the glider as it slides down the sand hill and takes off.

What was the next big step?

Wilbur and Orville began to build an airplane powered by a gasoline engine. The new plane looked like a glider — but it had an engine. The engine was connected to two propellers with extra-long bicycle chains. The engine turned the chains

The Wright brothers' airplane is ready to be tested. Notice the small gasoline engine on the bottom wing, the two propellers and the two rudders in the back.

and made the propellers turn. The spinning propellers would push the airplane forward. When the airplane was moving fast enough, it would lift up into the air.

The Wright brothers made the wings the same shape as the glider wings — curved on top, flat on bottom. The stronger air pressure

under the wings would raise the airplane and keep it in the air.

Propellers are built like the wings of a glider or airplane. The front of the propeller is curved, like the top of a wing. The back side is flat. As the propeller spins, the slow-moving air behind the propeller pushes hard. The fast-moving air in front pushes less hard. The stronger push sends the airplane forward.

When was the brothers' first planned flight?

On December 14, 1903, Wilbur and Orville were ready to fly. They put down a 60-foot (18 m) wooden track on the sand. On top, the men placed a small cart with wheels. Gently, they set the airplane on the cart. The plane, which they had named *The Flyer*, would take off from this track.

The brothers tossed a coin to see who would fly first. Wilbur won. He climbed in and lay, facedown, in the middle of the lower wing. The spinning propellers pulled the plane along the track. It was a great moment. But the plane did not lift up! Instead, it slammed right into the sand. Wilbur was not hurt. The plane was hardly damaged.

Wilbur had tried to make the plane rise too quickly, they thought. Their next job was to fix the plane.

The front view of the Wright brothers' 1903 plane, *The Flyer*.

What happened on December 17, 1903?

The Wright brothers tried again. The morning was very cold and windy. Neither man was dressed for the weather. Each wore his usual outfit — suit, white shirt, tie, and cap.

Wilbur ran alongside, as Orville became the first person to fly an airplane. Notice the narrow take-off track.

At 10:35 A.M., five friends helped Orville and Wilbur get the plane ready to fly. Now it was Orville's turn. He lay down and started the engine. It coughed and sputtered loudly. The propellers spun around faster and faster. Orville let go of the wire holding the plane. It started to roll forward. Wilbur walked, then trotted, and finally ran alongside. *The Flyer*

rose up into the air.

The machine wobbled and swayed. But Orville got it under control. It flew 120 feet (36.6 m) — about half the length of a football field. The flight lasted only 12 seconds. But it was the first time a human had ever flown in an airplane.

Did Orville and Wilbur become famous?

At first, very few people knew their names. But the brothers kept working — building better and better airplanes. Within five years, their planes could fly for more than an hour. They could travel more than 100 miles (160 km).

In 1908, Wilbur went to France to show off their latest airplane. Finally, people took notice. Everyone around the world wanted to learn about this remarkable new invention.

The brothers opened an airplane factory in Dayton. Soon, they were making two planes a month. They sold planes to the governments of France, Germany, England, Italy, and the United States. The brothers soon became rich and famous.

An airshow in France.

What did the future hold?

Wilbur died first, on May 30, 1912, in Dayton. More than 25,000 people came to his funeral. In 1955, he was elected to the Hall of Fame for Great Americans.

Orville, on the other hand, continued working for the next thirty years. Without Wilbur, though, Orville accomplished only half as much. His most notable invention was a seaplane that could take

6¢

FIRST FREE
CONTROLLE
SUSTAINED

UNIT

Delivering mail over long distances was one of the first uses of the Wright brothers' airplane. This stamp was issued in 1949.

off and land on water. After that he worked on other inventions — an improved bread toaster, a water pump, and a washing machine. Orville Wright died on January 30, 1948.

What are jet planes?

In 1939, engineers built a new kind of airplane. They called it a jet. Jets have special engines that burn jet fuel. The burning fuel forms a hot gas. The hot gas takes up lots and lots of space. It rushes out through a small opening in the back of the engine. As the gas speeds out, it pushes the plane forward. Jets can fly higher and faster than propeller airplanes.

This is a U.S. Air Force fighter jet plane.

Try it out!

Experiment #3: Use a small balloon to see how a jet engine works.

You will need a balloon.

1. Blow up the balloon.

2. Hold the neck closed with your fingers.

3. Now, let go of the balloon.

The balloon flies away! Why?

The balloon is like a tiny jet engine filled with hot gas. The air inside the balloon needs a way to escape. It rushes out through the opening of the balloon at high speed. This sends the balloon flying. It is much like the gas rushing out the back of a jet engine, pushing the plane forward.

How else have airplanes changed since 1903?

Today's planes are made of aluminum and steel, not wood and cloth. The biggest can carry hundreds of passengers over very long distances. The fastest can travel more than 2,000 miles per hour (3,200 kph). Most modern airplanes fly from 6 to 8 miles (9.6 to 12.9 km) above the ground.

Wilbur and Orville would be amazed and

The double-decker Airbus A380 is the world's largest plane with a wingspan of 261 ft. 10 in. (79.8m), length of 238 ft. 8 in. (72.75 m), height of 79 ft. (24.08 m), and 555 seats.

This jet fighter plane, the SR-71, was developed more than 30 years ago and is still the world's fastest and highest-flying aircraft. It can fly faster than 2,000 miles an hour (3,200 kph) and reach heights of 16 miles (25.7 km).

delighted by airplanes today. They may look very different from *The Flyer*, yet they are basically the same.

The brothers would surely want to fly in a modern jet. They would be thrilled at the rush down the runway and the liftoff. They would enjoy the view from high up in the air. And, no doubt, they would smile to think they had started the great Age of Flight!

Wright brothers time line

April 16, 1867	Wilbur Wright is born near Millville, Indiana
August 19, 1871	Orville Wright is born in Dayton, Ohio
Fall 1878	Brothers get toy helicopter and become interested in flying
1886	Wilbur helps care for his sick mother; decides not to go to college
1886	Orville starts printing business while still in high school
1889	Brothers open printing store
1892	Brothers open bicycle shop
1896	Otto Lilienthal dies in test glider crash; brothers become serious about building a flying machine
July 1899	Brothers test design for flying machine with giant kite
1900–1902	Brothers build gliders and test them at Kitty Hawk, North Carolina

Fall 1902	First truly successful glider flights
December 14, 1903	Wilbur attempts first flight in powered plane; crashes in 3 ½ seconds
December 17, 1903	Orville makes first successful flight in powered plane; lasts 12 seconds and travels 120 feet (36.6 m)
October 4, 1905	First really practical Wright airplane; flies for 33 minutes
May 22, 1906	Brothers receive patent for their airplane
May 14, 1908	First airplane flight with two on board
December 31, 1908	Wilbur sets record with 2 hour, 20 minute flight in France
August 2, 1909	U.S. Army buys a Wright plane for military use
November 22, 1909	Brothers start Wright Company to build more planes
1911	A Wright plane is flown from New York to California in 84 days with 70 stops
May 30, 1912	Wilbur dies in Dayton, Ohio
January 30, 1948	Orville dies in Dayton, Ohio

Index

Photo Credits: CORBIS: 1, 4, 10, 20–21, 25, 27, 47; Special Collections and Archives, Wright State University: 6, 7, 8, 9, 14, 46; The Granger Collection, New York: 16–17, 32, 40–41, 47; Underwood & Underwood/CORBIS: 19, 46; Science & Society Picture Library, London, England: 21; Library of Congress, LC-W851-121 DLC: 22; Library of Congress, mwright-04003: 30; Library of Congress, LC-W86-24: 34–35; Library of Congress, LC-W861-24 DLC: 36–37; George Hall/CORBIS: 42; Getty Images: 44, 45.

Berger, Melvin. • Can you fly high, Wright Brothers? : a book about airplanes / Melvin Berger, Gilda Berger. • p. cm.—(Scholastic science super giants ; 1) • ISBN-13: 978-0-439-83378-3 • ISBN-10: 0-439-83378-7 (pbk.) • 1. Wright, Orville, 1871-1948—Juvenile literature. 2. Wright, Wilbur, 1867-1912—Juvenile literature. 3. Aeronautics—History—Juvenile literature. 4. Aeronautics—United States—Biography—Juvenile literature. 5. Wright Flyer (Airplane)—Juvenile literature. I. Berger, Gilda. II. Title. III. Series. • TL540.W7B465 2007 • 629.130092'2—dc22 • 2006044257

18 17 16 15 14 13   14 15/0

Printed in the U.S.A. 40 • First trade printing, October 2007
Book design by Nancy Sabato